LOVE DURING LOCKUP

The Unfiltered Truth about Prison Romance

DOROTHY "DOT" PLYBON

ISBN 979-8-89345-739-1 (paperback)
ISBN 979-8-89345-740-7 (digital)

Christian Faith Publishing
832 Park Avenue
Meadville, PA 16335
www.christianfaithpublishing.com

Printed in the United States of America

This book is based on love during a locked-up experience that I had personally with a locked-up inmate. While certainly a learning curve spiritually and emotionally, I wish I had read this book first as I might have rethought my journey based on my goals in life. My journey started in 2015 and, unfortunately, ended in 2021. This experience was based in Florida, so the content of this book is based on facts witnessed in the Florida prison system.

Thank you to all my friends and family who put up with the highs and lows of my journey. Thank you for loving me through it all and the support you all gave. I am in great hopes that my journey will help someone else avoid any heartache. Be blessed.

CONTENTS

Introduction..vii
Chapter 1: To Engage or Not to Engage 1
Chapter 2: It's Just a Heartache...2
Chapter 3: Do They Really Love You?..................................5
Chapter 4: Conjugal Visits and Sex? Yeh Right! 7
Chapter 5: Did You Catch Them Cheating?........................10
Chapter 6: The Dime's on You...12
Chapter 7: Phone and Emails...16
Chapter 8: To Visit or Not to Visit 19
Chapter 9: Baby, It's about Me...22
Chapter 10: For You Kissers Out There 24
Chapter 11: Shaving 25
Chapter 12: But, Baby, I Gotta Eat....................................26
Chapter 13: The "Dear John" 28
Chapter 14: You Faithfully Waited.....................................30
Bonus Material...33
Florida Prison Slang 35

INTRODUCTION

I'm just a normal girl who experienced love with someone locked up. It is not my intent to bash or criticize anyone in lockup, as I have met some very wonderful people. I hope that my experiences and information will help those contemplating this type of relationship. I'm trying to give you the whole picture of what you can expect and endure with this type of relationship. This book is for anyone contemplating a love while in a locked-up relationship.

These relationship realities have been seen, discussed, documented, and experienced by me and other people who have been allowed into the Florida prison system. All of those who gave their thoughts about this topic certainly wished they had access to this information prior to their relationships with an inmate who was locked up, myself included. Much of the information obtained for this book was obtained by actual inmates who lived in it!

My journey started about twelve years ago, when I met a man named Gary Scott Rucci, aka "Rev," who was a prison minister at a local church singing event. Gary told me how he and his friends would ride their choppers into the prison yard and minister to all the prisoners, even ones on death row. Gary asked if I would be interested in going with the women into the prisons. I didn't even know much about a prison, much less jump into going to one. As curious as I became, I soon learned what prisoners go through and how they can overcome with Jesus Christ! I became more interested and even got to see Gary witness to others and bring them to the Lord. Gary's story started as a child at about twelve years old. Brought up under the influence of a motorcycle club and the Mafia, Gary began to share with me what Christ has done for him and how that old world and his testimony now help others to realize that the past they thought they had doesn't matter to Jesus! Jesus loves us through it all and still loves us no matter what. Monte Johnson, aka Snake, was another inmate who had shared his story with me of how he ended up in prison and served nearly (two) decades. It was only his faith in Christ that kept him alive! If you could only hear his testimony, you'd say, "That man must have had a praying momma and grandma for sure," and yes, he did! Chaplain Ray is another well-known prison minister who helped get Monte Johnson and countless other prisoners onto the righteous path in the prison system.

As a child growing up, I was always taught to stay away from anyone in trouble. Yes, we had a couple in my own family that had run-ins with the law and did prison time, but it wasn't discussed. I want everyone to know what this life is about and what it means to be involved in the transformation and forgiveness processes of it all.

Chapter 1

TO ENGAGE OR NOT TO ENGAGE

In this chapter, I will try to show key points to help you understand your potential role as an inmate's partner, but the ultimate decision is yours. The relationship between you and your inmate will affect all the people in your life. Your friends and family will see the highs and lows of the never-ending emotional rollercoaster of a life you will have.

Seek counsel and continue wisely. It will do the body good! No pun intended, but the closer you are to your inmate, the more you will yearn for them. Not being able to have physical relations or even regularly seeing them can take a huge toll on your health. This book is aimed at helping you realize the relationship while they are imprisoned before release or if they simply are not getting out.

I wish you all reading this the best of luck in your relationships. A lot of great people are locked up in prisons for a mistake they made. Learn the difference between a mistake and a Con game that all kinds of people learn to play. There is a difference between doing the crime and just wanting to make it through serving time and learning a lesson rather than just being a con who never learns a thing.

Chapter 2

It's Just a Heartache

When you fall in love completely and find yourself having to endure prison time with your inmate, things start to become clearer, and a lightbulb will go off. A litany of concerns will tumble through your mind.

What am I doing? He told me things to lure me, and the reality is far from what he originally said, but now I'm in love. Confusion and concerns have set in. You want to be held and cuddled at night! You want to enjoy the physical part that comes with a relationship. Where's your inmate when a loved one passes or is sick? Who's picking up the pieces?

Yes, they are there for you on the phone or in person one day a week or so if you are lucky, but what about the other things going on in your life? What about their expenses?

What about the time that it takes to keep things alive on the phone? You talk about normal things, but what about sex and intimacy? What about your sacrifices to keep this thing going? That's no real relationship. What about having to explain yourself while living your life on the outside? You went to the store, and you didn't answer their call. Now you must explain your time away day after day. There are a lot of jealous folks out there. Insecurities are at an all-time high with inmates.

Do you want your child to visit that prison every weekend? When you are visiting the prison, you become a prisoner of sorts and are part of their world for the day. Your kids will become so acclimated that they will feel at home and could one day become prisoners themselves. They may see their surroundings as no big deal. After all, the visitation area is one of the safest areas in the prison.

Speaking of kids, they will get attached to your inmate. They do not understand why your inmate is not at their ball games, but instead, they must visit your inmate in prison. Are you going to sacrifice your time with your kids? Please do not tell your kids that your inmate is at work. Kids are smarter than you think and, after time, will have it all figured out.

Many inmates want you to be behind bars to make them feel better or something. I tell you these things because I've lived it. My ex-inmate told me he would be out in two months. It turned out to be an extra eight years. That lie turned into a divorce. A divorce because I did not seek enough counsel or listen to my peers before I got married to someone on the inside. I do not dwell on the things or time I lost. I hope to turn this chapter of my life into a testimony to make others aware of the reality of this kind of relationship.

This life works for a lot of people; unfortunately, not many make it or are happy with this kind of life. Dealing with this type of relationship can also cause your kids to harbor hard feelings. My kids never liked the idea of me spending all my hard-earned money on something they always felt wasn't real when I was struggling just to make ends meet myself out here. Your extended family may even disown you because of the inmate's past. These feelings can certainly continue well after your inmate has gotten out. Inmates will not always tell you what is going on outside of the visitation. Sometimes, they will not allow you to visit. Don't take it personally. Sometimes, they are dealing with waves of emotions and just don't want to be seen in the place in their life that they are in. Inmates are dealing with having been beaten up that week or having been raped! That's right, sex is a daily occurrence. You either fight your way out of it and be left alone, or you just get so tired and worn out from years of fighting that you give up and give in. That's a tragic truth, for sure. Inmates often share a cell. That usually means a two-four-man cell with one bunk on top of the other. Best not to be claustrophobic as it's not a hotel room. Another inmate may be living in an open dorm with (one hundred) or so other inmates. This means no doors or walls. Just an open room with beds everywhere. You hear every conversation, thought, rage, and frustration of everyone in the room. There is absolutely no privacy in any of the surroundings. No crying, as it appears weak. Inmates think of how they've failed their families. How can they not be there in any of the daily happenings in your lives? You will have to learn to listen and read between the lines in their letters. Upon release, a good majority of inmates experience PTSD and must seek counseling. They can't sleep or have nightmares so bad that they fight in their sleep, even after years of being out of prison.

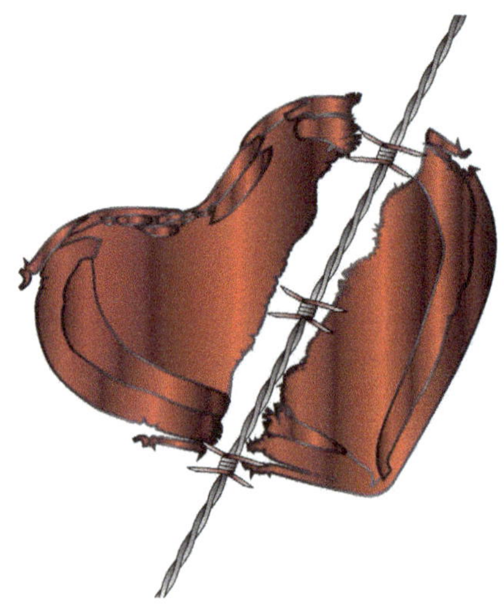

Chapter 3

DO THEY REALLY LOVE YOU?

What I experienced was spiritual manipulation. My inmate used the word of God to keep me full of fear and manipulated me into staying in the relationship. In the King James Bible, Hebrew 13:3 says, "Remember them that are in bonds, as bound with them; and them which suffer adversity, as being yourselves also in the body."

While I certainly understand and sympathize with some in prison, it is not a crime that I am convicted of nor doing the time for. I was constantly reminded of the bible passage, Acts 9:3, and how Saul was on the road to Damascus, and God stopped him, convicted his heart, and healed him. He thereafter was known as Paul. I know and believe that folks can change with God's divine healing and grace. But then again, some are cons, and they will do anything to have a friend, lover, or someone who can support them.

Here are some of the lines that may be used to entice or guilt you into a relationship. More things to think about as you explore your new relationship.

- Baby, I have never been in love like this before in my life.
- Baby, let's get married now. You are all I want!
- Is that all the money you got? What are you spending your money on?
- I can't do this time without you!
- I have no family but you!
- Baby, you rock my world like never before.
- Where have you been?

- Baby, she/ he is just an old friend who writes from time to time; they mean nothing.
- I have nobody to send me money but you!
- We are going to rock the world together when I am out!
- Remember what the bible says!
- Finally, I will kill myself if you leave me.

Chapter 4

Conjugal Visits and Sex? Yeh Right!

Conjugal visits are allowed in only a few state prisons across the country. That means the right to have physical relations with your married partner is almost next to nothing. When considering an inmate as a partner, it would be wise to have this conversation at once! I have researched each state online and can give you a quick idea of which states have conjugal visits in State prisons. I did not call each prison to check this out, and I recommend that you do your own research to reverify. This information is as of the writing of this book.

Only five states in the United States seem to have some type of program for Conjugal visits. They are Mississippi, New York, California, South Carolina, and Minnesota. Again, please check your state to get the most up-to-date information.

Okay, let's be real. There are NO conjugal visits in the Florida State prison system that I know of as of the writing of this book. So if you are a nymphomaniac and want to remain faithful, then you might want to consider the length of your inmate's sentence and figure out if this type of relationship will work for you.

While you normally get to get a kiss and hug at the beginning and end of your in-person visits, other ways of touching have been seen and well tried. Anything other than a kiss and hug can get your visits ended permanently or suspended for several months.

I used to say that they should get a lottery system for going for a free day out with their loved ones without supervision. Boy, wouldn't that make everyone really behave in there?

When I first started visiting my inmate, I saw mayonnaise packs being kicked around on the floor. Mayonnaise goes well on hamburgers but also has multiple purposes, as they do not sell "lube" in prison. Somebody was trying to get lucky that day somewhere! I will never eat a packet of mayonnaise again without thinking of its multiuse. Yuck! Again, sex is not allowed in prison, during visits, or at any time! I have heard of guys climbing walls and landing down in the bathrooms, which led to sex with their girls. That certainly was a rare case, as most buildings have walls that are sealed between the bathrooms. One time, the power went out in the visitation building. The groping was on, and the guards were freaking out, trying to get the lights back on. I mean, you do what you can when you can.

Sex in prison brings me to visitation, aka "VIZO" babies. Yes, babies born of conception at visitation do happen. Inmates will try anything and have been doing it for so many years that they have perfected the art of sex right in front of you. Women will change their clothing and watch the guard rotation, and when that split second comes up, it's game on for a quick "cop a feel" to your partner. People don't care if they get caught or are in front of kids. Some inmates are in there for life, so they don't care. Adding more sentences because they had sex doesn't matter. Their partner, however, may get arrested or charged and taken off visitation permanently. That would be for the administration to figure out and charge.

For your sex freaks out there, remember this: The guards will *not loan you their handcuffs*! So don't think you are going to get your freak on with handcuffs!

Chapter 5

DID YOU CATCH
THEM CHEATING?

This is an especially important topic. Inmates in prison often use this opportunity to have extra visit time, food, or just company, and they will do anything to obtain it.

You can have regular visits. Beware of your inmates when they keep asking what day you will be visiting. Your inmate may have a girlfriend or boyfriend on the outside, and you do not know anything about it.

I have seen an inmate taking the girlfriend and her son out very quickly as the wife made a surprise visit. Truly not funny, but they do it. I saw a young guy who had five different women visiting because they all had children from this guy. All are in love with him and now have torn hearts because they will raise their kids virtually alone. Shared visitation in this situation was not accepted by all the women.

Quite a few inmates are incarcerated and want to become better people, so they keep their noses clean while on the inside. Because of their desperate situations, others truly become *cons*. The CON will even *con you* to get whatever they want. They will even try to get close to the staff of the prisons to make their lives easier. Prisoners usually do not want that kind of stuff going on.

Besides extra visit time, food, and company, inmates try to get contraband into the prisons. Contraband can be things like drugs, phones, cigarettes, food, pictures, and things that are sharp to make weapons, aka shanks out of. Think of contraband as anything not on an approved Department of Corrections visitor list or allowed for purchase by the inmates themselves. Drones flying over prisons have also been caught dropping these types of contraband into the prison yards. The inmates involved usually get caught because the ones running to the pickup are usually the ones who ordered the drone—just shaking my head here. I can just picture this.

Chapter 6

THE DIME'S ON YOU

With your loved one in the big house, *you* will be the one footing all the bills. Most inmates do not have a way to earn money legally. Inmates often have an inside hustle, which would earn money that the inmate will use to trade for things they need on this inside. A side hustle is simply a way to trade or barter with someone else's goods or services that they may be able to offer to help the inmates support themselves without asking you for extra money. One hustle might be *sex*. Other hustles might be passing messages for food. Another might be doing law work for people as the inmate may have been trained to do legal work on the outside.

Jailhouse lawyers are available. Most have been trained to help with motions, appeals, and yes divorces. These lawyers are trained and certified to help with the simplest of legal work. Quite a few of them are that good and can get people out of prison, but it does cost. Will the legal help cost you? Or will your inmate figure out a trade on the inside?

Overall, their hustle will not help *you*.

You will be paying for those one hundred calls a day if your inmate is a talker. Hope you got a silent one! You will be paying for commissary (anything sold by the prisons to inmates) so that they can have extra food, toiletries, drink, snacks, etc. Food and snacks are not priced well. They usually pay about what you would pay on the outside.

The three hots and a cot that you hear about are really three colds and a one-inch pad of rubber to sleep on. The calorie intake is so low that it keeps people very sluggish and malnourished. The food is of mediocre quality. So anything to help with supplements is always appreciated. Funding your inmate will be like having two households to support!

You will be asked to help with their case by doing things such as visiting lawyers, filing their motions, or being asked to help reopen their case as they didn't do it! Going to guess that very few are *not guilty*!

Does your inmate have debts? Good credit score? You will be encouraged to help repair all these types of things because your inmate will want to come out and start their life over as if nothing happened. Your inmate will want to eat out, drink, and party. Who's going to pay for that until he gets a job? Getting a job requires transportation, clothes, toiletries, and incidentals. The expense of having your loved one at home can be burdensome. Both of you cannot live off love alone. Upon release currently, inmates receive an automatic $100.00 gift from the State of Florida prison system and a bus ticket, so be prepared.

Also, currently, the State of Florida prison system charges inmates a total of $50.00 per day upon release for every day they were incarcerated! Yes, just happened to someone I know. He went to pay court fines so that he could be squared up with them, and they made him sign a payment arrangement for more than $246,000 to pay them back for the housing and food that he received from them while incarcerated. There must be a better way to resolve this before release because most inmates must work in the prison as if they had an outside job. They must work without pay, and any excuse is not usually tolerated. So if the prison is saving money by not hiring folks from the outside, how is it fair to charge someone all this money on the outside upon release? What a way to set up someone for failure, and certainly, it will raise the return to prison statistics!

Okay, You Decided to Be in the Relationship

guilty
of love
P.D.230573

Chapter 7

PHONE AND EMAILS

So your loved one is incarcerated. How do they have contact with the outside world? Their world has now been turned upside down. For those text, phone, and email junkies, tell them to just breathe! There are a few things afforded to them, but most inmates are in the hope they have people on the outside who want to support them so they won't be as limited while locked up. Cell phones are considered contraband. Getting caught with it will reward them with a new room called the confinement room or lock up. If caught, they may get several days to think about things in confinement, or they can simply be sent to another prison. If confined, you are not allowed to leave the tiny room to which you are confined. You are in there by yourself. You are allowed two showers per week and food. Confinement has very harsh conditions. It's hot in the Summer and extremely cold in the Winter.

Outside of confinement, inmates are allowed normal living conditions if you call no air conditioning or windows with no airflow normal. Inmates are allowed phone calls if they have money in their account to pay for them. They can email if they want money again to pay for the emails. They do not get a discounted rate! They pay full price for everything! I currently believe inmates in the Florida Prison system get one five-minute free call home per week.

Please remember to check carrier rates for phone services. They vary quite a bit. The best way to get the best rate is to talk to other families while you wait to get in to see your loved one and compare rates. Trust me, you will see the same faces over and over and over until their inmate gets out or is transferred. Many good friendships are made while waiting to get into visitation among those not incarcerated.

Remember, if you get aggravated or want to hang up on your inmate, you can, if you decide to, block the number from the prison. You can do this, but keep in mind that it is hard to unblock. Blocking and unblocking may cause a loss of phone privileges because the phone company doesn't like to keep reactivating the phone number so that it will go through. So if you decide to block the call, make sure you don't want any more calls. Trust me, I know. Tried this out once.

Please remember that all calls are always recorded. If you have something juicy to say, it is recorded. If you talk about someone else, it is recorded. If your loved one wants phone sex, it will be recorded, and sometimes your inmate will allow another inmate to listen by allowing the other inmate to eavesdrop on the call just to get a honey bun pastry that's sold in the commissary! Inmates must stand so close in line for phone calls that conversations can be heard without even trying to allow someone else to listen. With that in mind, if you want to have sexual fantasies over the phone, such as taking your man to the *car wash* and fantasizing about what you can do inside the car before the car wash is done, remember, it's recorded. The guards called out an inmate and visitor once over this, letting them know what they heard. LOL (Laugh out loud), inmates will get called out and harassed. All calls are recorded, and the guards listen to them. Your privacy in life is over. Emails are also checked. Don't try and talk in code. It is checked. Just don't. You never have full conversations as everybody else is listening in or monitoring. There are room mics and guards all over listening. Never talk about your case unless you want it public knowledge.

Chapter 8

To Visit or Not to Visit

Okay, so now you have decided to make that first visit a reality. Please be flexible and have an open mind. A lot of things happen when you visit. First, there is the ride to the prison, tolls, and gas. Hook up with another visitor to help with the travel costs, as you will have tolls and gas costs to think about. When you get to the prison, they may have you wait outside or, if lucky, inside. Waiting outside would include waiting in the rain or wind. Many facilities have a waiting area for visitors, but the prisons I visited do not. Wait times can be two to three hours, depending on who is in charge that day or if anything of a security risk is being checked out. Dogs are often used to check out the vehicles that come into the prison compound parking lots. Dogs are often used to seek out drugs that are being smuggled into visitation.

If you do not like crowds, it is best you do not go to visitation.

When you get inside, you must check in. Take off your belt, shoes, hats, and sweaters and place them on the conveyor belt in a bucket. No purses are allowed, just your approved items in a transparent plastic coin purse. Make sure that your sexy self is not wearing any camouflage or white shirts or anything that would cling or show your cleavage. Camouflage and white shirts are forbidden because inmates wear white T-shirts, and prisons are afraid someone could change clothes and allow the inmate out during a visit. For the camouflage, if an inmate were to have access to camouflage and manage to escape, the camouflage clothing would function as camouflage and make it harder for the prison to catch the escaped inmate. Children are also not allowed to wear these types of clothes. Women do not wear underwire bras. The prison views the underwire as a weapon, and wearing one could cause your visit to end.

Once you are lucky enough to get through the front door, you then must check in with the control center. Please present your ID and inmate-approved number. Makes it easier. For God's sake, call and make sure you can visit your inmate before you visit. The Florida Department of Corrections website lets you now see if your inmate is locked up or has had their visitation suspended. Your inmate could be in trouble and now in lockdown or sick or something. Good to also call to make sure that you are on their list of folks that have been approved to visit, and it's a go for the visit.

After you wait in another line to get in, you must declare everything you are wearing, such as the number of earrings, belly rings, barrettes, watches, rings, jewelry, etc. You come in with the same and leave with the same things you wore. *Do not* let your inmate handle anything that you have on. They could get disciplined as anything you have on them is considered contraband.

Don't try and smuggle a dang pork chop in your hair! No lie, I have seen it. Don't send Granny with a skirt to smuggle contraband up under her skirt. Everyone is checked. They have guard dogs that will sniff you down during check-in. If a dog sits down in front of you, just know you are going to get strip-searched, detained, or arrested, as that dog has detected something on you.

Once all the above is done and you pass to get in, the girls will go to the girl's waiting area to once again pull the bras up to shake them out, and the guard will check shoes and do a pat down. Pat down does involve the guard running hands up between your legs and down to check for anything weird. Just think about what the inmate must do. It's no joke. If they do not do what they are told to do, no visit is allowed. Most want a visit so badly they would not do it, but they do a complete strip down on inmates, and they must do a bend-over prayer and hope they were not trying to smuggle in something. A few guards try and become proctologists. Yeh, disgusting and scary. I was at visitation one day, and the inmates were coming out and all disgusted and told everyone that the guard was cavity-searching their butts with a flashlight to make sure they had nothing to hide. That is *usually not* what an inmate should expect. This guard was reprimanded for his behavior that day. Once the inmate has been cleared, they will enter the visitation building where they can meet their visitor.

One day, an inmate got caught exiting the visitation room and had the following lodged in his *exit only*: two cell phones, two cell phone chargers, and an ounce of the drug K2. It was not a good exit for him as he incurred extra charges, and was transported to another prison.

Make sure you follow visitation rules. Your visits are subject to approval and can be revoked at any time.

Chapter 9

BABY, IT'S ABOUT ME

You are visiting your inmate. Give your attention to them as much as possible. I love talking to people, so for me to sit elbow to elbow at visitation drove me crazy. Conversations can be quite hilarious, and you cannot keep from hearing them as they are often loud and funny. In time, you might learn to tune out the noise around you, but for me, I just couldn't tune it all out.

For me, on the outside, I have to multi-task daily with phone work and people coming in the door and acknowledging them both. In a room full of people at the prison, I can see who is coming and going from the room, the conversations, and who visited who last week. It gets interesting when different people come and romantically visit the same person. Observe, but do not ask.

In the rule book, it says not to speak to other inmates. You just cannot help it. Sitting so close to people, you just cannot help but talk to other inmates and their visitors. So with that said, your conversations are known. Be careful, as somebody sitting next to you may be hearing you and or reading your lips and then telling your business. Are they undercover? Rule of thumb: trust *nobody*!

If you are eating food and have leftovers, please let it be known that you are willing to give your food to other inmates because many inmates do not have funds for extra food, or some are just that hungry. Your scraps are valued by a lot of inmates in there.

If a person sitting next to you is just that irritating, try to be rational. If you can't be, don't hit them. You will get arrested. Try to wait for another seat to open and *move*. If there is a serious situation, alert the guards. Please have compassion for those mothers who visit their children every week when they know their kids are not coming home. I've seen elderly parents visit knowing it will be their last visit due to their old age or illness or driving distance to visit. A mother and father's torment for sure.

Chapter 10

FOR YOU KISSERS OUT THERE

Kissing or touching of any kind is extremely limited. You are allowed to greet your loved one and hug or kiss briefly. A real *bummer* if you like to kiss. Any tongue action better be hidden, or consequences may arise from the correction officers. You'll figure out how to make it count. A brief kiss and hug are also allowed in many prisons when the visitor is leaving. If your exit hug and kiss are too long or elicit, consequences can include things such as verbal warnings to the inmates. Repeated warnings can result in a disciplinary report. This usually takes place away from the person visiting, or a reprimand can be either friendly harassment or not, such as the infamous room searches. Room searches can be done for no obvious reason, or simply to communicate power and control by completely throwing your room upside down.

Your inmate can lose your papers, pens, clothes, food, etc. just for no reason. Oh yeh, no cameras installed to keep anyone accountable in most dorms. It's their word against the guard and your inmate will usually lose. The guard controls the inmate's life in everything they do or think!

Chapter 11

SHAVING

Shaving before you receive a visitor is usually needed. Gutter mouth and muck pit are not good. You must always keep closely shaven. If you tend to grow hair quickly and like your beard, well, you might have to get another style or be in the barber chair most of the time. Barber services are not *free*, and you will have to arrange a way to pay or trade for services. I heard an inmate say to another inmate that his girlfriend showed up for visitation, and her leg hair was longer than the hair on his head. That was funny. You just had to be there.

It depends on who's on duty as to whether you can get a slide for your hair at visitations. Some guards are ruthless and want the hair on your head gone, and some let you get by with a little longer. It's rare.

If you come in with long hair, it will be short for the entire duration of your nice and friendly stay with the Department of Corrections.

Chapter 12

BUT, BABY, I GOTTA EAT

As I said before, the inmates usually get three colds and a cot. They are afforded the opportunity to buy items out of the prison commissary. They are only allowed to buy a limited number of things on one visit. They must count their items and know exactly what they have in their account to pay for them. Commissary visits are *not* guaranteed. Certain situations will have the prison on lockdown, so this privilege is at a halt until the situation is solved. It's always a great idea to have snacks on hand in case of a lockdown. Sometimes lockdowns can last for days. Food and snacks are not priced well in the commissary and often can be much higher than what we pay on the outside. Ramen noodles are a dollar a piece versus what we can get out here sometimes for half that price. Water is a dollar a bottle. So you see, the prison is also there to make money.

As a visitor, you are allowed to enjoy lunch with your inmate if you like when you visit. Commissary and lunch can run a good $30.00 to $40.00 a visit if you both eat throughout your visit. That amount can also include a photo if you choose to capture the moment with a color glossy picture taken and developed by one of the prisoner camera guys. Visitors will often eat before they visit to cut down on the cost and just have a drink with their inmate and pay to have them eat. YOU DO NOT GET GRILLED FOOD! You may be able to buy things that you can heat up in a microwave or just vending items, period!

Most inmates look like they are starving. Food is a privilege there. They do not have the luxury of opening a fridge or cabinet for

26

food anytime they want, like we do out here. They are looking for the crumbs!

Chapter 13

THE "DEAR JOHN"

Of the time spent with your inmate and everything that goes with it, time will tell. Did a healthy relationship form between you and your inmate? Was it a fight constantly? Financial drain? Physically draining on both parties from stress and having to keep up both parties? Life with an inmate can be a living hell on the outside! Every situation is different and certainly based on the sentence your inmate was given as to how long you can hold on. With that said, you may one day get the "Dear John," as we call it.

The "Dear John" can be a final notice given by either party, be it by email, phone, letter, or any other means available. It's the break-up notice. Your relationship is completely broken and done.

Inmates think about this every day. When is that day coming because my significant other can't be faithful, or have I been? Is it time to let them live on the outside, free and happy? I know someone who was locked up and in an incredibly happy relationship. She was the love of his life. After giving it much thought, the inmate broke off the relationship due to his long prison sentence, and in her best interest, it was his wish that she live on the outside free, happy, and able to have a real family with kids. After they broke it off, she eventually married on the outside and had a family with kids. The decision to give the "Dear John" is one of the hardest things in life, especially if you are truly in love and want what's best for the other person. Breakups are hard whether in prison or not, and most certainly do pull at the heartstrings of everyone involved.

After receiving a "Dear John," inmates will often consider things like suicide, give up on behaving, and get stupid crazy, and some will risk getting killed trying to escape and will be drastically affected in some way or another without any doubt.

The friends or family of the inmate who got the "Dear John" have severe ill feelings toward you. Your inmate may file child visitation rights. You may be threatened with retribution upon your inmate's release because your inmate knows you are going to be with another person on the outside and happy while your inmate is suffering a nightmare from hell. No matter what, you will always be blamed, no matter who was at fault, the crime, or the amount of time in prison. Even if the family holds ill feelings toward the inmate, blood relations will trump anything you've done in most cases.

My "Dear John" was when I filed for divorce. My inmate lost his mind. He went crazy and just couldn't function for a long time. He lost his financial and emotional security and everything he could hold onto as I was his link to the outside world. My inmate will be getting out soon, and I do fear retribution in some way. I am not looking forward to having to watch my back constantly in the future.

Chapter 14

You Faithfully Waited

Upon your inmate's release and having endured all with them, the love of your life is finally released. Your love is now in the free world with you, and you expect to live happily ever after with each other. Well, there are other aspects you may not have known or have forgotten. Your beloved significant other becomes an ex-felon and, with a felony charge, can drastically be challenging when trying to find work or housing.

There are countless employers that advertise that they will hire felons until you apply. They do scrutinize the offense and take that into consideration before offering work. Quite a few companies will not hire ex-felons for any reason. Some welcome them with no problem based on their prior crime. Big corporate companies will not allow ex-felons to even be dishwashers or even flip burgers based on criminal and sex offender background checks. That's right, two separate background checks at most places. Depending on the crime decides your inmate's ultimate outcome of employment unless they go into self-employment. The ex-felon status will devastate an inmate in several ways, even in a profession that your inmate may have held prior to going into prison. Remember, all civil rights were taken away when your inmate went to prison, and most of all, rights will not be restored upon release.

Things will be ten times worse if your inmate's prison sentence is a sex offense. If it was, your inmate must be on a sex offender registry for life. Every time you and your inmate move, that registry must be updated. Failure to do so could land your loved one back in prison. Your inmate must show proof of residency at each move and the new location in which they live. They will not be allowed to live near a school, park, or even a residential area. If you have kids, your inmate will be barred from school events, causing you to have to explain to friends and family why they can't join in for the event. Both of you will suffer consequences that you did not anticipate.

Landlords are even more strict when it comes to felons. Some do, some don't, and some just won't rent to a felon, period! I hear some ex-felons wait years to get a place to live and or work, depending on their crime. I've always said that if folks knew what a prisoner had to endure just to make sure they make it out of prison at the end of their sentence, they would *gladly* give them a job and housing!

Now your inmate is free as a bird and has not had sex in a long time. Is the jailbird going to stay with you because of your dedication and faithfulness, or is he going to fly elsewhere?

Just something to consider. I've seen some fly upon release, and others die because they can't take it on the outside and have heart attacks or were ill on the inside and needed so much medical care that they just passed from being ill for so long.

Please be aware of the locked-up type of life with your significant other or the one you met during correspondence and phone calls, in there and upon their release. It could be the greatest thing in the world, living happily ever after forever, or you might be running into strife, which creates a nightmare of a life you didn't anticipate. I pray my book gave you guidance to really decide what you are going to do with your *locked-up love*.

BONUS MATERIAL

You might have been in prison if as follows:

- If you get caught in the middle of the night staring straight up in your bunk at the stars, you might have been in prison.
- If you clean the toilet inside and out every time you use it, you might have been in prison.
- If someone notices you taking a one-minute shower, you might have been in prison.
- If you put a hungry man's dinner in a microwave with a fork and it blows up, you might have been in prison.
- If you walk straight from your front door, right down to your driveway, twenty feet down the sidewalk, then you nervously look up and down your street before taking two steps onto your grass to pick up your newspaper, you might have been in prison.
- If the nurse walks into the waiting room and yells your name, and you stand straight up at attention, say your former ID number followed by "ma'am," you might have been in prison.
- If, while seated in your favorite restaurant, you stop the busser to pick scraps off discarded plates, you might have been in prison.
- If your whole family sits down for holiday meals, and you try trading or bartering your food servings with others, you might have been in prison.
- If you must use the bathroom at home and someone else is already using it, you knock on the door and say, "I've got it next," you might have been in prison.

- If you and your significant other sit down in a restaurant and, upon looking at the menu, you say to them, "How much money did you put on my card?" You might have been in prison.
- If your significant other or anyone accidentally drops their keys, book, wallet, etc., and you refuse to pick it up for them as you're thinking *contraband*, you might have been in prison.
- If you carry your own roll of toilet paper both into and out of your own bathroom, you might have been in prison.
- If you completely inhaled your four-course meal at an elegant dinner and jumped up to leave in less than five minutes, you might have been in prison.
- If your idea of cooking dinner involves single servings of ramen noodles, assorted bags of smashed potato chips, and onions that you picked out of your salad at lunch, you might have been in prison.
- If you constantly drive five miles under the speed limit, you might have been in prison.
- If you take a walk with your significant other, and you can't walk faster than one to two miles per hour, you might have been in prison.
- If asked where the mayonnaise is, you might have been in prison.
- If you are in a car at a stop sign and you start to smell gas fumes and you panic and say you are going to die from the gas fumes, you might have been in prison.
- If you turn on the computer and wait for AOL to boot up and make the connection sound, you might have been in prison for a long time.

Florida Prison Slang

*Common knowledge terminology in which
your inmate lives and has to adopt!*

- Bit: Term of prison sentence.
- Blue Bird: The inmate transport bus.
- Blues: Prison attire.
- Boo Game: Trying to intimidate an inmate with violence.
- Bootie Bandit: Forcibly commits rape upon unwilling inmates.
- Boss: A term used by inmates to refer to officers who are also guards.
- Brogans: Prison-issued boots inmates must wear.
- Buck of Hooch: Home-made Alcohol.
- Buck Rogers Time: Prison sentence with parole extremely far in the future or Long term.
- Bunkie: Cell roommate.
- Bunker Down: Get in your bunk and get ready for bed.
- C/O: A correctional officer and another name for guard.
- Cadillac: Cigarette butt can.
- Cage: A prison cell.
- Catch a ride: Contact high off someone else's drugs.
- Catch the Wall: An indicator that you need to get into the corner to fight.
- Chesters and Diaper snipers: Child Molesters
- Chin check: Punching an inmate in the jaw to see if he'll fight back.
- Choke sandwich: Peanut Butter sandwich without jelly.
- Chow: A prison meal.

- Classification officer: Helps an inmate with everything they need in prison. They arrange cell assignments, transfers, jobs, time left, and other personal matters.
- Commissary: A place where inmates can go to buy incidentals that are allowed by the prison system. Inmate pays for this.
- Contraband: Anything not issued to an inmate by the State Prison system.
- Count time: Being physically counted by the prison three to four times per day.
- DAP: A prison greeting, aka fist bump.
- Dear John: A letter to an inmate showing the termination of a relationship with their significant other on the outside.
- Dime: A ten-year prison sentence.
- Doobie: A hand-rolled marijuana cigarette.
- DR: Disciplinary review in writing.
- Drop a slip: Snitch on another inmate by reporting them in writing by placing the paper in a box requesting aid.
- Dry Snitching: Ratting out another inmate by talking loudly about their bad behavior in front of prison staff.
- Eat your lunch: Means the fight is on.
- Eyeballing: Somebody is looking at your property.
- Education: A place inmates can go to get their GED or college classes.
- Fishing line: Made from torn sheets or string. Used to throw down the run of cells of inmates to other cells.
- Funky: An inmate that does not bathe and often smells.
- Gen Pop: General population with all inmates. No inmates are secluded from each other in this area.
- Going Psych: When a prisoner shows signs of severe mental illness such that they need to be moved to a Psych ward.
- Green Light: Permission to kill a person or gang affiliated on sight.
- Gunne/Snippen: Masturbating while looking at somebody or something, usually in plain sight.

- Homeboy: A prison clique marked by extreme and blind loyalty. This group may have lived near each other on the outside.
- Hospital Corners: An extremely specific way to make up the corners of your bunk.
- Institutionalized: Inmates who can no longer live in a free world. Someone who no longer functions on the outside by themselves.
- Jody: A man sleeping with an inmate's wife/girlfriend on the outside.
- Keister: A body cavity to hide contraband, usually in the buttocks.
- Kite: A contraband note written and folded and passed to others.
- Kitty: Term used by male inmates for a female correctional officer.
- Lame duck: A weak inmate standing by themselves in the prison yard.
- Law library: Used by inmates to help with legal matters.
- Library: Used to check out fictional and non-fictional reading books.
- Lifer: Has a life sentence without parole.
- Lockdown: Any kind of disturbance that causes prison staff to lock up all inmates in their cells until the disturbance is cleared up.
- New fish or fresh meat: In a men's facility, this is the term for a new prisoner. New to prison politics and how facilities are run.
- On paper: A term for being on probation.
- One time: Warning that an officer is coming.
- Playing on ass: Playing or gambling without money. If you lose, you pay with your body.
- Protective custody - Special confinement area for prisoners in fear of their life from the general inmate population.
- Psych Ward: Mental Health Ward.

- Rabbit Blood: Someone who has it in his blood to escape prison and will take every chance to escape and doesn't like confinement.
- Reckless eye balling: Inmate staring at a female or female officer.
- Rips: Hand-rolled cigarettes.
- Road dog: A close inmate friend who may have become friends on the inside or were friends on the outside.
- Shakedown: When a prison staffer rips apart a prison cell looking for contraband.
- Shank: Homemade weapon made of anything that will cut, stab, or cause bodily harm.
- Shut eye: Sleep needed.
- Sissy: Gay inmate who volunteers to have sexual relations.
- Slam Dunked - When a guard has forcefully tackled an inmate to the ground to be detained.
- Sleeve Up - Term for having numerous tattoos.
- Strapped - When an inmate carries a shank or shiv aka homemade weapon.
- Taylor made: Manufactured cigarettes.
- The hole: Solitary confinement due to disciplinary actions.
- Tighten up: An indication that you are about to fight.
- Turned out: An inmate that has been forcibly sexually assaulted. Once this happens to someone, it's expected to keep happening.
- Warden: Top official in charge of the prison.
- X'd out: When an inmate's days are limited due to a hit put out on them to have them killed.
- Yard open: A nickname for a fenced in area for outdoor recreation used by inmates.
- Zoo Zoos and Wham Whams: Another term for sweet treats like cookies and candy.

About the Author

Dorothy is a new and upcoming inspirational author. Being newly retired from the insurance field after thirty years now gives her the time that she needs to write a sequel to follow. Dot was raised in the South most of her life, and she is a straight-up type of person, which leaves her writings very relatable and not sugar-coated. Although a humorous person by nature, she is humbled by being a mother and grandmother and spends her spare time with her grandkids and family, who are dear to her. Writing country gospel songs is a big passion of hers and a huge form of praise in her life. On the weekends, you will find her on the back porch with coffee in hand, just listening and watching for all the sights and sounds of every waking creature. To Dot, it's about the simple things in life.